MY WILL
OR
HIS WILL

LEARNING TO LIVE
A LIFE TO SURRENDER
SECOND EDITION

MY WILL
OR
HIS WILL
SECOND EDITION

STEFANIE AUSTIN

Edited by River Walk Publishing, LLC

PUBLISHING, LLC
San Antonio, Texas

My Will or His Will
Visit our website at MyWillorHisWill.org

Request for information should be addressed to:
Stefanie@mywillorhiswill.org

ISBN 978-1-7344974-2-7

e-ISBN 978-1-7344974-4-1

Library of Congress Control Number: 2020923717

Electronic Version:
Amazon Kindle Publishing

Professional Editor:
Christopher C. Herring, River Walk Publishing, LLC
www.RiverWalkPublishing.com
Thank You Stefanie Austin for teaching us how to live
God's Will.

Printed and bound in the United States of America

ACKNOWLEDGEMENT

A special thank you to my Lord and Savior for placing the thoughts to write this book in my heart and mind to share with the world. The people that inspired me along the way have been my great grandmother who taught me to pray and read the Bible as a little girl, my grandmothers who were and are God fearing women, great aunts, loving parents, my children, siblings and my tribal community.

Thank you all for being there for me and my family throughout the years and for years to come.

FOREWORD

Stefanie is a very incredible Christian women, who have trusted God in every step of her life journey. I have known Stefanie for more than 20 years. I find her to be loving, kind, and trustworthy.

I have seen her overcome so many obstacles in her life, but she didn't let them hold her back. Because of Stefanie's strong faith in God, she kept moving forward, counting her setbacks as a comeback to even greater testimonies on how great her God really is in her life.

Stefanie let God speak through her in the inspirational writings of "My Will or His Will" to reach others who are going up the rough side of their mountains.

She is helping them to find Hope, Joy and Peace in the comfort of her loving Savior.

I believe Stefanie's motto is "If I can help somebody as I travel along, then my living will not be in vain."

I know you will enjoy her inspirational devotionals, because I and so many others have found fresh bread from her writing.

In Christ,

Pastor Melvin Preston
Family Ministries Director at South Atlantic Conference of Seventh-day Adventist Greater Atlanta Area

Spiritual Nuggets
Learning To Live A Life To Surrender

INTRODUCTION

"My Will or His Will" was birthed out of trials and tribulations that I was going through in my life. I've been married, divorced, and single. And during each of those phases in my life, I have had plenty of moments of joy, and my share of sorrows. As a single mother of three daughters, it has not always been easy. Juggling my work as an executive, active servant leader in the church, and the day to day demands and duties as a mother came with many sets of experiences that led to this book. My journey as a novice writer was not apparent to me when I was sending out daily inspirational messages to family and friends; when the messages were intended for me. I learned how much God truly loved me during those valley moments. He would always find a way to connect, inspire and minister to my weary and sometimes worn soul.

I have come to learn that God's voice is clearest when we are still. Over 10 years ago, I began journaling and keeping spiritual nuggets that I would send to people, and the responses I received were surprising. God would have me to share inspirational nuggets with a few people, which then grew to 10, 20, 60 and eventually sharing it on a larger social media platform.

Many times, people would say, "this was right on time, and thank you for sending this to me when I needed it the most." I was often asked by others, "how did you know that I was going through this very thing?" My response would be, I did not know you were going through anything, as many times God directed me to share this spiritual inspiration or either I was going through the situation myself.

I would send early morning text messages because that is when God would speak to me, and I could hear His voice clearly. I was often asked, "when are you going to write a devotional?"

I did not give it much thought because I was sharing what God had placed upon my heart. How many of you already know that God does not place something upon your heart just for you? He knows that you are not alone on your journey and that others could benefit from the lessons too.

God impressed upon my heart to write a women's devotional, and in my conversation with Him, I went back and forth with my will versus His will. I told him that I was going to write a devotional for men and women.

Well, when you want to see God laugh, just tell him your plans. In telling God what my plans were, I heard his voice less, regarding daily devotionals. You see, the devotionals weren't anything that I decided to write. God Almighty always inspired my writings, so I just couldn't make it all up. Over the years, I would continue telling God what I was going to do. I would tell him my will, and God would share with me His will. After going back and forth and enduring many bruises, I finally surrendered.

Ironically, the title God gave me was "My Will or His Will". How appropriate, because all along my will was to have a devotional for men and women, and God's will was for this devotional to be for only for women, so I thought. Actually, God wanted me to relinquish and do what He instructed me to do, which is "Learning to Live A Life To Surrender". When I yielded, He instructed with me to share the book with everyone. The lesson was that the devotional is for all. The purpose was for me to surrender to my Heavenly Father.

I have been a servant leader in church well over 20 years, a mother of three beautiful daughters, and a healthcare executive, but the role that brings me the most joy is serving God. I hope that this devotional, *My Will or His Will*, will speak to your situation, encourage, and inspire you, while providing practical insight in following God's will for your life. May it also remind you and others to press on and never give up hope.

Stefanie Austin

14

TESTIMONIES

During my challenging battle with breast cancer, Stefanie's spoken words of comfort, breathed life, uplifted me and opened my heart so that I could receive overflowing realms of possibilities in magnificent abundance. Her words of encouragement were and continue to be a result of my healing.

I am forever grateful for our sistership, and that she honors and is obedient to God's will for her life.

Patryce L. Sheppard
Founder, Faith in the Fight,
Awareness & Education

TESTIMONIES

Stefanie

Your love for God, your character, and your heart inspire me to be better. Blessed to have you in my life, Sis.

Thank you for always being your authentic self, never wavering in your beliefs, and always taking the time to encourage others.

I'm praying God's grace and mercy, along with his abundant blessings as you embark on this new journey!

Love you to life, Sis!

Carolyn Webster

.

"Over the last ten years, I have been incredibly blessed to be included in Stefanie Austin's morning devotions. What Stefanie did not know, she would send me the right words and the right scriptures at precisely the right moment. Those words helped me make it through some rough situations that were very stressful and at times, were very dark. Stefanie's devotions have inspired my family, friends and coworkers when she touched on different topics such as God's love for us.

Stefanie's heart is so close to God's Word. It is evident in every devotion she shares. Stefanie's gift, which she graciously shared with a few, has made room for her to share with many."

Proverbs 18:16

I am so proud of you!
Forever your Sister,

Jacqueline Duncan

17

"I have known Stefanie for over twenty years now, and she has always been an inspiration to everyone. She is a natural encourager. Her devotional has the power to uplift you and to bring you out of your dark places. God has truly blessed her with this gift.

I was going through a rough time in my life. One day I felt overwhelmed and awoke in the morning to receive a text message from Stefanie about how God had given her a word about staying encouraged no matter how tough and hard things seemed. She shared her own testimony about how she was able to overcome a difficult time in her life and what helped her. This made me feel encouraged to know that someone else understood and wasn't ashamed to voice it to help someone else. I felt much better and was able to later share it with others."

"Stefanie continue to go forth in your gift that God has given you! I love you!"

Wanda Floyd

One of Stefanie's devotions in "My Will or His Will" took me back to when I was growing up without the presence of my biological father. This was due to my parents ending their marriage when I was in elementary school. My fathers' absence impacted me more when I became a teenager.

I am thankful for my praying mother, who planted a seed of hope in my two sisters and me. She told us that we could go to our Heavenly Father anytime to ask for protection, encouragement, guidance, etc., and that He would never leave or forsake us.

"My Will or His Will" has encouraged me on several occasions. Thank you, Stefanie, for allowing God to lead you!

Love,

Delia Williams

1. My Will or His Will?

My Will or His Will? Who struggles with that? I know I do. We say, Lord, let Your will be done, but we find ourselves stepping back in our own will. Could this be a test to see if we really mean let Your Will be done, Lord?

The Bible says, "the spirit is willing, but the flesh is weak." I always applied that scripture to a sexual connotation, but the scripture applies to much more to include how we react to one another in sadness, anger and happy times. God didn't say it would be easy, but this is where our faith is tested, which is another challenge.

We must truly surrender our all to God. The devil (Satan) doesn't want us to experience the true meaning of God's love and power. I'm determined with God's will, to trust Him, have faith in Him, and for God to change my sinful ways.

We all have sinful ways and some of those ways include getting in the way, trying to do it without God, and getting so angry with someone, you want to "lay hands" on them. But remember, the change must occur in you.

John 5:30 New King James Version (NKJV)

I can of Myself do nothing. As I hear, I judge; and My judgment is righteous, because I do not seek My own will but the will of the Father who sent Me

2 Corinthians 5:7 New King James Version (NKJV)

7 For we walk by faith, not by sight.

2. Are You Teachable?

Are you teachable? What does that mean? Think about learning spelling words. You first must sound out the letters. Then try to pronounce the word and look up the definition. Additionally, you will need to study the words daily so you can remember how to spell it. Teachers will also ask the students to use the word in a sentence to show the proper mastery of their newly added vocabulary word. When you look at the many steps just to learn a new word, that takes commitment.

God is the same way. He is our first teacher. Are you committed to God teaching you His ways? Are you willing to put in the time and effort? God is the instructor, and we are the students. Allow our loving Father to teach you!

Psalms 32:8 (NASB): *I will instruct you and teach you in the way you should go. I will counsel you with My eye upon you.*

3. Keep My Mind Stayed On You

Keep your eyes and mind on the Lord. How am I angry and irritated with people when my eyes and mind are on the Lord? I'm not saying we aren't human and that we should operate like robots. What I am saying is when we are caught up in the moment of our flesh, how quickly do we turn our eyes and mind back to God so that we won't stay angry? I'm guilty of being angry at the core about situations. However, I'm pleading with God to keep my mind on Him and telling my sinful feelings, "No!"

Isaiah 26:3 New International Version (NIV)

You will keep in perfect peace those whose minds are steadfast, because they trust in You.

4. Help My Unbelief

Lord, thank you in advance for allowing me to press through any situations that come my way. You wouldn't allow me to be in this place at this time if you didn't think I could handle it. Thank you, Lord, for reassuring me day in and day out. Lord, remove those people who don't have good intentions. You know who they are, and I pray that you will convict their heart and soul.

Let me press through this path you have me on and thank you for my spiritual brothers and sisters you continue to have in my life. Help my unbelief. Hallelujah!!!!

Mark 9:23-25 New King James Version (NKJV)

23 Jesus said to him, "If you can believe, all things are possible to him who believes."

24 Immediately the father of the child cried out and said with tears, "Lord, I believe; help my unbelief!"

25 When Jesus saw that the people came running together, He rebuked the unclean spirit, saying to it: "Deaf and dumb spirit, I command you, come out of him and enter him no more!"

5. What's In Your Heart?

I remember singing this song several times in church, but I really didn't appreciate the song until I got older. There are so many things that we allow in our hearts and minds, and do we really take time to invite God into our hearts daily? In order to have a change in mind, I believe we must have heart surgery.

Here's the song I'm referencing:

Into my heart, into my heart
Come into my heart, Lord Jesus
Come in today, come in to stay
Come into my heart, Lord Jesus

Psalms 51:10 King James Version (KJV)

10 Create in me a clean heart, O God; and renew a right spirit within me.

6. Troubled About Things?

This morning I lie in bed thinking about things and ask God questions. I think about all that's going on in my life, and I wish I could fix everything that's going on. Do you ever feel this way? Many times, we wish we could fix things at home, work, friendships, relationships, financial things and family, but we don't have the power to do so. However, we do have God. I've been told that prayer changes things, but I realize that it doesn't mean that it changes things in your favor. Prayer changes your heart to accept what God has planned for you. It is easy to say stop worrying about things. It seems a lot harder to actually do it, however, our Father instructed us for to quit worrying for a reason. One, He wants us to give everything entirely to Him and truly leave it there. Two, God knows that the devil wants us to worry so that we can lose faith in Him, and finally, He wants us to lean not to our own understanding. Pray and ask God to help you stop worrying about tomorrow but trust Him every step of the way.

Matthew 6:34 (NIV)

34 Therefore do not worry about tomorrow, for tomorrow will worry about itself. Each day has enough trouble of its own.

7. Are You A Friend or A Foe?

Many times, we have people in our lives who say they are our friends, and as time goes on, we see they really weren't our friends. Some have used the term "acquaintance." Well, I know things aren't always black or white, but for the protection of your personal space, an acquaintance should not have the privilege as a friend. A very close friend shared with me on several occasions that it's important to invest in the "emotional bank," with friends. My mother used to say a dog that brings a bone takes a bone. Instead of trying to figure out who the people are in your life that might fit the above description, my question is, what are you to the people in your life? If you are a foe, remove yourself from that person's life. There's not anything good you're depositing into the relationship. If you realize you want to contribute to a healthy friendship, then be that true friend. Pray about it and seek God's wisdom. It's sad when we don't realize what we genuinely are to people.

My prayer is Lord, remove me from people's lives if I don't have good intentions and help me to be honest in my self-evaluation. Are you for that person or are you against that person? Pick a side.

Joshua 5:13 (NKJV)

13 And it came to pass, when Joshua was by Jericho, that he lifted his eyes and looked, and behold, a Man stood opposite him with His sword drawn in His hand. And Joshua went to Him and said to Him, "*Are* You for us or for our adversaries?"

8. Sinner Saved By Grace

As a Christian, I make mistakes, and sometimes I make choices to sin. We can fool ourselves to think that we are not intentionally sinning; however, the only person you're fooling is yourself. There are times that I say God will forgive me, and He will, but I must not take Him for granted. I'm not saying to allow the devil to hold you hostage in your sin and to beat yourself up. What I'm saying to myself is that I'm a sinner and God, please help us sinners to resist temptation and not allow anyone to talk us into sin. Have thine own way, Lord. I thank God for His grace and mercies.

Psalms 41:4 (NKJV)

4 I said, "Lord, be merciful to me; Heal my soul, for I have sinned against You."

9. Life Distractions

Life has its ups and its downs, and many times we forget all that God has done for us. Many times, our blessings are right in front of us, but we can't see the forest for the trees, meaning life's distractions. As I thought about that, I was able to connect with this character in the Bible, Elijah.

Elijah's faith was very strong in the Lord. God revealed himself many times to Elijah and performed miraculous things. Elijah's faith was strong, but when Jezebel killed the prophets and threatened to kill Elijah, he became afraid and ran.

I've asked this question, why did he run when God has shown him that He will protect him? Hasn't God has done many powerful things? Elijah's fear and anxiety blinded him, and many times, those emotions take over or blind us from God. The devil continues to pull or trick us into this cycle. The question is, how do we come back to the source, which is God?

Prayer has worked for me, and my friends who love the Lord have encouraged me. Sometimes we get so blinded by the trees that we don't see the forest or the blessings that are right in front of us or the miracles God continues to perform. Take a step back when these emotions overtake you. Seek out those who truly encourage you in the Lord. God never changes. He's the same yesterday, today and tomorrow.

Kings 19:9-11, 15, 16 (NIV)

9 There he went into a cave and spent the night. The Lord Appears to Elijah And the word of the Lord came to him: "What are you doing here, Elijah?"

10 He replied, "I have been very zealous for the Lord God Almighty. The Israelites have rejected your covenant, torn down your altars, and put your prophets to death with the sword. I am the only one left, and now they are trying to kill me too."

11 The Lord said, "Go out and stand on the mountain in the presence of the Lord, for the Lord is about to pass by."

15 The Lord said to him, "Go back the way you came, and go to the Desert of Damascus. When you get there, anoint Hazael king over Arm.

16 Also, anoint Jehu son of Nimshi king over Israel, and anoint Elisha son of Shaphat from Abel Meholah to succeed you a prophet.

10. Get Back Up

Lord, you know our heart and that we desire to serve You. We're not perfect, and we make mistakes that only you knew we would. In our shortfalls, we recognize that we need to keep our mind fixed on You. When we stumble, Lord, please forgive us and keep us close to You. The world has no authority in judging us. We present the judger to You to deal with Lord. We desire to serve You, and as we walk this life's journey, we may stumble, but Lord, we are getting back up, still choosing to serve You. Thank you for loving us all despite ourselves.

Psalms 37:24 (NKJV)

24 Though he fall, he shall not be utterly cast down; For the Lord upholds *him with* His hand.

11. Only By The Grace of God

I have made it through, and it's only by the grace of God and the prayers of my family and friends.

There are times I am getting ready for work or driving in the car, and God and I will have our time to talk to one another. As I review my past or my current circumstances, God shows me how good I have it and have had it for a long time. All I can do is shout hallelujah and thank God for where I am in my life.

I know the old saying, "You can't see the forest for the trees," but I am experiencing it now in my spirit. I felt it yesterday and having an open heart to hear what God has done and is doing is a breath of fresh air. I was driving yesterday, and it was about to rain cats and dogs! I saw the storm coming, and as I looked up, God reminded me, I am with you even in this storm like I have always been. Don't let your past or current situation keep you there.

The devil is trying to steal what God has just for you. It's okay to be sad, angry, mad, or disappointed, but open your heart, soul and mind to the Word of God. That is your strength, your nourishment, your food. God made YOU to be a witness, and we are His vessel. You are not alone in this walk!!

Deuteronomy 31:6 (NIV)

[6] Be strong and courageous. Do not be afraid or terrified because of them, for the Lord your God goes with you; he will never leave you nor forsake you."

12. God Speaks To Us Daily Through Nature

Nature has so many lessons that we take for granted each day. There are lessons from a caterpillar all the way to the king of the jungle, the lion. God speaks to us through nature, and I must say when I'm sitting on my porch or walking on a trail, I see and hear God's voice. I believe the devil keeps us so busy that we miss God speaking to us. I remember a point in my life when I was in a dark place, and God would come every morning and serenade me with a little bird singing outside my window. At first, I used to say, why does this bird come and wake me up every morning? Go away! But when I started talking to God in prayer and took a moment to pause in the morning, I realized it was God serenading me. I noticed how beautiful the grass was in my backyard, even though it was brown. God revealed to me that things would die, but new beginnings will come. I had a garden and watched how a small seed grew into something magnificent and how it needed to be watered to grow, just like we need to water our soul daily.

God, thank you for not giving up on me. You are my rock and my salvation. Whom should I fear? No one!!!!!

Psalms 96:11-12 (NLT)

11 Let the heavens be glad, and the earth rejoice! Let the sea and everything in it shout his praise!

12 Let the fields and their crops burst out with joy! Let the trees of the forest sing for joy

13. Move Out of The Way

When a person tells you that I'm going to pray and ask God how to interact with you, that's a blessing. It's even more of a blessing when they truly want to do what God wants them to do versus themselves. Many times, our flesh gets in the way of so many things in life, work, children, relationships, friends, and even strangers. It's hard to relinquish all power to God. We say that we want God to lead, but we take the reins from Him all the time. We say we want a man to lead, but we step in front unknowingly.

I wonder if there is a message from God to us to seek Him first and move out of His way? Is this a lesson that He's teaching us so we can follow in other situations? Not only relationships with a significant other but even in our interactions with friends, family, church members and other things.

I think the hardest struggle in life is to move ourselves out of the way. Lucifer was so in love with himself. He had selfish motives, even now this is true. How selfish are we in wanting what we want and not wanting what God has instructed us to do?

Jeremiah 29:11 (NIV)

11 For I know the plans I have for you," declares the Lord, "plans to prosper you and not to harm you, plans to give you hope and a future.

14. Tempted, Who Me?

Jesus was tempted when he was in the wilderness. As humans, we are all tempted. Sometimes people act as though they are not, but we are tempted every day, whether it's big or small. (i.e., lying, gossiping, cursing, stealing, cheating, being deceitful, tearing down one another, etc.) The takeaway from Matthew 5:10-11, for me, was when Jesus resisted the devil, angels came later and ministered to Him. Can you think of a time you resisted temptation, and God worked out the situation or provided something better for you? We all fall short, and God has great plans for us. When temptation comes our way, let's tell the devil to flee in the name of Jesus.

Matthew 5:10-11 NKJV 10 Then Jesus said to him, "Away with you, Satan! For it is written, 'You shall worship the Lord your God, and Him only you shall serve.'" 11 Then the devil left Him, and behold, angels came and ministered to Him.

15. Silver and Gold

Does silver or gold fulfill your inner soul? Some would say yes because they are content and don't have a care in the world.

Some people don't have bills, and want for nothing, yes, silver or gold fulfills my inner soul. Really?

Let us look at history in the Bible and even wealthy people today. People enjoy their fame, riches and bling. You can't take your riches with you when you die.

If we chased after God like we do for wealth, education, love, we would be rich in Spirit. There's nothing wrong with wanting the best. If we would put the same amount of effort in seeking God, just imagine where we would be.

Matthew 6:33 (NKJV)

33 But seek first the kingdom of God and His righteousness, and all these things shall be added to you.

16. Even Jesus Needed To Be Encouraged

Many times, people don't know how to encourage others or believe they don't need to encourage someone because they appear to "have it all together."

There's a book that's called the Five Love Languages, and I believe this book isn't only relevant for romantic relationships, but it's also relevant for any relationship you encounter with people.

Some people need a word of encouragement, a touch, a small gift of encouragement, spending time with a person in order to encourage them, acts of service, or just prayer.

Jesus needed His disciples to stay up and encourage Him in Gethsemane, but they couldn't stay awake. Even though He was Jesus, He still needed the encouragement from his Father.

We all need encouragement. I ask you, do you now how to encourage your fellow man or woman? You must know their language to encourage them.

Prayer is always beneficial. However, there are times a person needs just a little bit more of something else. Explore what that could be.

Matthew 26:38-40 (NKJV)

38 Then He said to them, "My soul is exceedingly sorrowful, even to death. Stay here and watch with Me."
39 He went a little farther and fell on His face, and prayed, saying, "O My Father, if it is possible, let this cup pass from Me; nevertheless, not as I will, but as You will." 40 Then He came to the disciples and found them sleeping, and said to Peter, "What! Could you not watch with Me one hour?

17. All That I Have

There is a song that resonates in my spirit for the Love of my heavenly Father that he has for me. It is by Andrae Crouch.

" All that I have I give to You, my Lord
And that's the least that I could do, my Lord
Long before I knew my name, You loved me
And You proved it all at calvary

The years may come and they may go, my Lord
But still our love will not grow old, my Lord
I could never last one day without You
You have a love so strong
A love so true

You're the song I sing
You're my everything"

God, I will continue praising You because You gave Your life for me. Life's situation or circumstances won't keep me from praying and praising You.

Thanksgiving for God's Righteous
Judgment

Psalms 75:1

We give thanks to You, O God, we give
thanks! For Your wondrous works
declare *that* Your name is near.

For the rest of my days, I'm going to sing
Your praise.

18. What Do You Desire?

In my reading this morning, God lead me to Psalms 51:10. I decided to read the entire chapter. Repentance was the theme, and as I meditated on this important chapter, the first section spoke about God having mercy on us. Sometimes we sin intentionally and keep moving as if it's nothing. There are some who sin and do not blink an eye because, in that person's mind, they do not think what they are doing is a sin. (i.e., gossiping, deceitful, white lie, etc.).

Do we repent at all on any sin?

David asked God to "Blot out my transgressions. Wash me thoroughly from my iniquity, and cleanse me from my sin. For I acknowledge my transgressions"

David knew the importance of repenting and acknowledging his sin. His desire was to be close to God.

What do you desire?

Psalm 51:10 (NKJV)

Create in me a clean heart, O God, and renew a steadfast spirit within me.

19. Loving Him With Everything

What does a loving God with everything look like? We always hear people remind us about the first commandment, "If you love Me, keep my commandments...." We understand it. However, sometimes, we struggle. How do we love God with our mind and soul? How do we make and keep Him at the forefront of our hearts and mind?

Our mind is the doorway or avenue for God to enter. How do we keep other things, other people, from occupying that space completely? God should have a front-row seat in every aspect of our lives. Sometimes we give jobs, children, people and other things that main position. Would someone say we are making those things our idols? I don't know, but today I say, Lord, I want to love you with my whole heart, body, mind and soul. Teach me to love you and keep you first always.

Matthew 22:37 (NKJV)

Jesus said to him, "You shall love the Lord your God with all your heart, with all your soul, and with all your mind.

20. What Do People See In You?

Many times, people will say I don't care what people think about me, I'm just going to be me. I understand that concept to a certain degree.

People have their opinions just like they did with Jesus when he was walking on this earth. At the end of the day, they said He was a healer, a teacher, a counselor, provider, performed miracles, and much more. Sure, they were ugly things said that were not true. Jesus continued showing mercy and compassion no matter what He was accused of. Jesus was a peacemaker.

When people speak of You, what do they see other than the materialistic things?

Do they see Jesus in you?

When you're upset, do they see Jesus in you?

What does your significant other, children, friends, coworkers, church members, strangers see in you?

Do you stir up trouble? Are you so aggressive that people question, where is Christ that is supposed to be living in you?

Lord, I ask that you show me my flaws and cleanse me on the inside and out. Help me to be the peacemaker even when it's not my fault.

Matthew 5:9 (NIV)
Blessed are the peacemakers, for they will be called children of God.

21. Show Myself, Remove Me, and Then Humble Me

There are times we lose perspective or have a false sense of who we are or what we are doing. We may think we have it all together because we know what we are doing at work, at home or even at church. We have our plans all laid out to the tee. Sometimes we tell ourselves I have been doing this particular thing for years. I can do it with my eyes closed. We get so full of ourselves that we don't ask God for help, even in the areas we think we perfected. Take time to ask God to show you, you. Meaning show me all my flaws, Lord, and help me to accept them and not deny them. Remove me out of my own way and help me to remove these flaws. As you remove me, Lord, humble me so I can be submissive to You as You lead me through life journey.

Remember when Nathan told David about the rich man poor man story, and how David was mad at the rich man taking the poor man's lamb. David was furious and said this man should be punished. David didn't realize that he was the man that did

this sinful act. Sometimes we don't realize how we sin against God when we do our own will. Yes, we can say it was blatant that David sinned, but isn't it blatant when we put ourselves before God doing our own will without asking God to let His will be done?

2 Samuel 12:5-7 (NASB)
5 Then David's anger burned greatly against the man, and he said to Nathan, "As the Lord lives, surely the man who has done this deserves to die. 6 He must make restitution for the lamb fourfold, because he did this thing and had no compassion." 7. Nathan then said to David, "You are the man! Thus says the Lord God of Israel. 'It is I who anointed you king over Israel and it is I who delivered you from the hand of Saul.

22. Shut Up and Listen

So many times, we have so much to say about a matter that's frustrating to us. We think that we have the right and the expertise, so we are going to say what we feel is right. I get so angry with myself because I know I have crossed this path so many times in my life, and God gives me scripture to try to guide me back on His path.

I continue to do things my way because I think that I'm the subject matter expert. It's like a hamster on the running wheel, who gets nowhere but back in the same spot. We ask ourselves, why do I keep having this same test?

My Pastor preached this past weekend about our issues we need to address before being in a relationship as well as friendships, and I say also working relationships. God is so kind with His Word because He says be silent. I'm telling myself, Shut Up and Listen to God. It also applies to those who are leading you at home, church and work.

Being submissive is a daily task, and it doesn't mean that you're weak. I look to my spiritual sisters and brothers to encourage me in the Lord, but to also hold me accountable. Sometimes we are our own worst enemies. I have only a few spiritual men and sisters that I seek counsel from, and I thank God for them.

Job 6:24 (NIV)
Teach me, and I will be quiet; show me where I have been wrong.

Psalm 27:11 (NKJV)
Teach me Your way, O Lord, And lead me in a smooth path, because of my enemies.

23. God's Touch

God wakes me up in the middle of the night at times, and I hear the quietness in the house and outside. I lay in my bed for a while and try to say a quick prayer so that I can go back to sleep. Then I begin to worry because I think that something is going to happen today. After one minute of worrying, I start to pray for my family individually, friends, married couples, single people, work, my job, leaders at church, enemies and anyone else I fail to mention. I then seek out the scriptures asking God to direct me to what He has for me. I begin to feel His touch in the Word. I know God is with me always. however, I feel His presence when He wakes me up in the middle of the night.

No matter what's going on in your life, know that God will not forsake you. Also, remember that He has a Word for every situation. Rise above your situation by placing your hands into God's hand, and you'll find that peace that surpasses all understanding, even during a storm.

Psalm 91: 1, 5, 11 (NIV)

1 Whoever dwells in the shelter of the Most High will rest in the shadow of the Almighty.

5 You will not fear the terror of night, nor the arrow that flies by day.

11 For he will command his angels concerning you to guard you in all your ways.

24. Let Come What May, I'll Be Okay

God is in control of everything, and we must remember that during the good and bad times. He only wants the best for us, and He'll do whatever it takes to shape and mold us.

When baking a cake, the ingredients aren't good to eat until all of them are mixed and baked. No one wants to eat oil, flour, sugar or a raw egg by itself, but when you mix all the ingredients to make a cake and bake it on 350 degrees, it turns out being delicious.

Going through the fire is painful, but God said I'll be with you always. I've always asked God for a mate that's my spiritual leader, provider, and protector. A mate who would encourage me, help me through the storms, and all along, I had it in Him. So, I say now, let come what may because I'm going to be okay. My loving Father, who is my friend, provider, protector, and spiritual leader, has my back, and there's nothing that will happen without His approval.

God knows everything, even before it's going to happen. As my pastor preached this weekend, praise God for your trials, which are a blessing to help you grow spiritually. So, during trials, we will suffer but praise God as we go through and come out on the other side.

1 Peter 5:10 (NIV)

And the God of all grace, who called you to his eternal glory in Christ, after you have suffered a little while, will himself restore you and make you strong, firm and steadfast.

25. I Can Only Imagine

When Daniel knew that he was being plotted against by the men who worked for the king, I can only imagine what was going through his mind. His action appeared that he wasn't worried because of His relationship and trust in the Lord.

When Esther heard what Haman was plotting to do, I can only imagine the anxiety she felt for her people and herself. However, her family member, Mordecai, instructed her to pray, fast, and wait on the Lord.

The other story that comes to mind is Job. The Bible shares his story and the struggle; however, he still loved the Lord in spite of his trials. I can only imagine how it made him feel.

Knowing that God is with us no matter what we are going through is comforting. The devil tries to keep us so stressed out so that we can't remember God's promises. Praise God and seek God no matter what.

Lord, we ask that Your will be done in our lives and give us the strength and whatever we need to accept Your will.

2 Corinthians 12:9-10 (NIV)

9 But he said to me, "My grace is sufficient for you, for my power is made perfect in weakness." Therefore, I will boast all the more gladly about my weaknesses, so that Christ's power may rest on me.

10 That is why, for Christ's sake, I delight in weaknesses, in insults, in hardships, in persecutions, in difficulties. For when I am weak, then I am strong.

26. Didn't Realize

Wow! Today was an interesting morning all before 11:00 am. As I went on with my day, I didn't realize how many things I did in my own will. Just the small things I decided I wanted to do. It seemed as though God cleared His throat and reminded me to consult with Him.

I knew what I wanted to do. However, I paused to ask God what should I do, and guess what? It was the opposite of what I was going to do. I ask myself; how can I make sure that I consult with God on the small and big things? I don't have an answer; however, for me, I'm going to be intentional and make that effort. God is concerned about every aspect of our lives, and sometimes we take for granted His willingness to direct our path. He's all-knowing, all-seeing and why would we not discuss all matters with the Master?

Ephesians 3:20-21 (NKJV)

20 Now to Him who is able to do exceedingly abundantly above all that we ask or think, according to the power that works in us, 21 to Him be glory in the church by Christ Jesus to all generations, forever and ever. Amen.

27. With Open Arms

Lord, with open arms, I thank you for your love letter, the Bible.

With open arms, I thank you for the treasure of wisdom, knowledge, patience, love, and a forgiving heart.

Thank you for the many life lessons you've allowed me to go through, which was a way for you to refine me.

I know my journey isn't over, and you have more in store for me.

Prepare my heart, mind, and soul for what is to come.

Help me to hear Your voice every day all day as I seek Your guidance.

Give me wisdom and discernment, Lord.

Amid chaos, I choose to hear Your voice.

Thank You for all that You continue to do in my life.

Colossians 2:2-3 (NKJV)

2 that their hearts may be encouraged, being knit together in love, and attaining to all riches of the full assurance of understanding, to the knowledge of the mystery of God, both of the Father and of Christ,

3 in whom are hidden all the treasures of wisdom and knowledge.

28. I Need to Find Myself

Sometimes we get lost in being busy at work, church, raising kids, family, spouse, or other things. We may sometimes lose ourselves and forget what the real purpose is for our life.

It is important not only to take time out for your family, work, and God, but you must still in way to regroup, reset or just recharge your battery. An engine can't run on its own without getting an oil change or transmission change. If those things are neglected on a car the car cannot operate appropriately. Can you remember a time that you ignored the warning signs of your body when you needed to rest or recharge? I can remember and it was not a pretty sight for my family, friends or even co-workers.

Take some time out of your busy schedule and find yourself. Seek God. He will help you find yourself and restore you to the place you belong.

Luke 11:9-10 (NIV)

9 So I say to you: Ask and it will be given to you; seek and you will find; knock and the door will be opened to you.

10 For everyone who asks receives; the one who seeks finds; and to the one who knocks, the door will be opened.

29. God's Love Is Unconditional

There's nothing we can do to stop God from loving us. Don't allow the devil to trick you in thinking what you've said or done keeps God from loving you.

God knew what we were going to say and do even before it happens.

God makes an escape for every situation. It is hard to see the escape when we are not connected or in tune with God.

God love us so much that He creates a space where we can retreat from our sin, but when we do not His word say, "repent and sin no more".

I love how our Heavenly Father loves us.

Isaiah 54:10 (NIV)

10 "Though the mountains be shaken
and the hills be removed, yet my
unfailing love for you will not be shaken
nor my covenant of peace be removed,"
says the Lord, who has compassion on
you.

30. Fiery Darts

Lord, there are days that life is wonderful, and I don't have a care in the world. I am singing and skipping with every step, but when those cloudy days come, I feel myself losing faith, asking what is this and why?

God, the fiery darts catch me off guard sometimes, and I don't know what to do other than cry and scream inside.

I know You are not surprised when these fiery darts come my way, and neither should I. Please help me stay close to You and your word.

Your promises in the Bible give me comfort and remind me that You're with me always.

Lord, I will submit and will be humble when these situations come my way.

I ask for the spirit of humility and faith. Show me, Lord, the lesson I'm to learn, and I praise You in these circumstances.

Thank You, Lord, for Your love and covering.

Ephesians 6:16 English Standard Version (ESV)

16 In all circumstances take up the shield of faith, with which you can extinguish all the flaming darts of the evil one

1 Corinthians 10:13 (ESV)

13 No temptation has overtaken you that is not common to man. God is faithful, and he will not let you be tempted beyond your ability, but with the temptation, he will also provide the way of escape, that you may be able to endure it.

31. When You Can't Stand Any Longer

In life, you take the good with the bad, and you keep on plunging forward. You've been that strong person for your family and friends; however, the attacks keep coming. Sometimes you feel like giving up, but you remember God's words in your head. You continue walking through life's journey and you wipe the sweat off your brow and say, Lord, this load is heavy. When you can't stand any longer, I say to "stand on God." Sometimes we forget that we need to be standing on Him all along. There's no judgement for that because we are human.

God says, "come to me those who are heavy burdened." He knew we would have heavy burdens. Sometimes people want to pretend that it's all good when it really isn't. It is okay to say this is too much for me, I need You Lord. When you can't stand any longer, take it to Jesus.

Matthew 11:28-30 (KJV)

28 Come unto me, all ye that labour and are heavy laden, and I will give you rest.

29 Take my yoke upon you, and learn of me; for I am meek and lowly in heart: and ye shall find rest unto your souls.

30 For my yoke is easy, and my burden is light.

STEFANIE AUSTIN
FRISCO, TEXAS
FACEBOOK
INSTAGRAM
TWITTER

**Find Stefanie online at
www.mywillorhiswill.org**

**On Facebook at
www.facebook.com/mywillorhiswill**

on Twitter @mywillorhiswill

and on Instagram @mywillorhiswill

Made in the USA
Middletown, DE
06 January 2021

30786263R00044